chimera

kaela prall

for the lovers, the monsters, the weirdos, the freaks,
and anyone who has ever thought they were too much.
you're exactly what the world needs and
i'm so fucking glad you're here.

chimera (noun)

1. a fire-breathing she-monster in Greek mythology having a lion's head, a goat's body, and a serpent's tail
2. an imaginary monster compounded of incongruous parts
3. an illusion or fabrication of the brain, especially an unrealizable dream

(Merriam-Webster)

all i want is for you
to see the soft
(and sharp)
parts of me,
know that they are good,
and honor them
even when they do not match
the picture of me
that lives inside your head.

−chimera

she is not yours.
her nurturing,
her gentleness,
her sensuality
were never meant for you.
yet you have taken them,
like gold from the cool earth—
you have pulled them out and hung them around your neck.
you take,
and take,
and take,
and wonder why she is tired,
why the light behind her eyes has faded.
you ask, does she not give?
is this not her purpose,
to water your garden
and heal your calloused soul?
everything you are missing is reflected in her stillness,
but she was not made for you.
her fields and mountains are for her to live upon.
her healing hands were given to soften the places
within her that you have hardened with your
pressing, begging, stealing.
your mouth is dry because you forgot how to whisper
your needs to the earth and instead began to take
beauty up by its roots.
she has not forgotten.
her hair is woven with rivers and flowers.

her tears are raindrops and oceans and stars.
the universe reaches out
to hold her
steady
while she balances the world in her hands.
all you have taken from her will turn to ash
in your mouth
and she will forget you
like a pebble under her foot.

−she already has

that is not a halo.
it is light refracted
through distance.
if you had the courage
to stand close to her,
(you don't)
you'd see the dirt on her elbows,
scrapes on her knees,
and pain in the lines
on her face.

−all the saints are dead

i am not made of flesh
but wrapped up in it,
hostage to this day,
blooming in countless tomorrows
and moments now passed.
fragments of light,
the smallest of threads
tighten around my tongue.

−let me go, let me go, let me go

if you must be afraid
(and we all must)

fear the sting of sleepless nights
next to someone who cannot love you.

fear every moment of freedom traded
for the comfort of familiar pain.

fear a life that holds you hostage
to its insatiable hunger.

if you must be afraid
(and we all must)

fear these, but
do not fear loneliness.

—choose wisely

pull it up by the roots.
burn the field and
mix the ashes with salt.
what you want
and what you need are
not so different after all.
each recipe claims
a pound of flesh,
your feeble soul
gasping for breath
in the baking sun.

−revenge

you cannot hold an ocean
in your hands.
(you should know this)
i will not whisper
because you hate to hear me scream.

-erosion

why does the heat of our anger surprise you?
you saw us soft and on our knees,
faces to the sun, at ease,
and chose to cast your shadow here.
we swallowed each of your cuts,
pleading with deaf gods
until we became more scar than flesh,
until we rose together from the blood.

now we are barbed and burning.
look on us with shame and see what you have done.
look into our eyes and know:
if we're going to hell, we're taking you with us.

—we are soft and lovely things no more

i will write about the dirt under my nails,
how i looked for the stars on new moon nights,
how i wept wordless into the wind and
prayed it would cease or take me whole.
i will write about the stones in my shoes,
the dust in my eyes,
the homes that i built in the dark,
how i willed it away and it always returned.

−i'll write it all/but not today

please teach me
what it means
to hold these roses
(to bleed)
and to live with them
under my skin.

—chronic

if i'm careful
        (gods, i'm so careful)
today will stay folded neatly,
pressed at the seams
and tucked away.
rest is a dream i'll have sometime in the night,
then i'll rise
        (eyes shut tight)
and do it all again.

—what am i missing?

above all
it is the space within that frightens me,
the echo of questions when i demand answers.
(why did i think i was a finite, earthly thing?)
i swear i tried
to make myself small,
to pass through this life unnoticed.
but the universe within
expands indomitably outward,
pushing through every forest and fence and hedge,
a cold gasp polishing mountains clean.
i will take the time to look,
but i don't know what i'll see.

—know thyself

i am begging,
(please)
wanting with an aching hunger.
why are there only crumbs at your table
when you promised a feast?

tell me where i misstepped,
where i wandered off the path
to now find myself so desolate.
you promised enough.

i wish i could live as the mouse in your cage.
i wish i was small enough to be satisfied with nothing.

−i am not

we stretched ourselves thin
across too many cold days.
put stones where
kisses should have been,
spoke only in half–truths
with arrows in our teeth,
turned giants into mites under our skin—
then broke in half under
the weight of what is
and what could have been.

–january love

i'm not here to
make you good,
to ease the pain,
to make you whole.
you look upon the field
and worry about its state
but have yet to put
your hands to the plow.
are you afraid this is
the one thing you cannot do?
that your hands aren't meant
for healing?

−i'm done asking

i always imagined
myself as the mouse
until i saw the damage
my eyes,
my mouth,
my heart could do.
i am the wolf,
teeth bared in the dark,
stealing moments with
the moon.
and i'm sorry
i had to love you
to know it.

−i thought i was the prey

you are here before me
(flesh and blood)
but i cannot feel you.
we are separated
by a universe of
unspoken desires,
lives built and unbuilt
in a moment.

−trying to love

i cannot yet weep for
this heartbreak.
its hands are still
around my throat.
i wish the ocean
would swallow me,
pull me deep into
the numbing cold.
let me fall asleep
and wake up to a
different world tomorrow.
let me dream
of a universe where
i didn't break your heart.

−*i'm sorry*

they've been buried
and i swore
i wouldn't go
looking
for them
anymore.

—pieces of us

when did the horizon
become a metallic beast?
tomorrow holds me in a gunmetal grip,
it drags onward, relentless,
no time for stillness of mind.
come, soldier, and face the straight
and narrow path to destruction.
we have no need for joy
in this machine.

−all your plans have been made

i cannot tell you my love for the sun
and the moon is the same.
i don't write for pleasure.
i write so there is someplace to hide
when the sun is hot and unforgiving.
i offer the moon a place between the lines
so you can pull it out
in the dark and find your way.
i bleed onto the page so i may wake again
tomorrow with some hope in my hands.
i never know if it's enough.

—invocation

the desert is gone
but there's still sand
in my eyes.
it clings to the edges,
presses in until i cannot tell
where it ends and i begin.
i soak in the springs
'til my skin
      turns gray,
drink from clear pools.
(do not come up for air)
there are some things
the rain cannot wash away.

−geography

no value can be placed on
the curve of your back
or the lines around your eyes.
you labor for rest
but they will not give it.
(i can see you from here)

the rattling beast is begging for your soul,
but you don't need to have it all.
plant yourself firmly in the shade
by a sweet, cool spring.
(bring a paradise)

−give only what you can without bleeding

i have emptied honeyed veins over and over,

carried splinters in my skin—

they told me i was born a martyr.

(lies i fed with my own flesh)

good intentions

thorned and vicious,

who am i if not a savior of the damned?

−i am the wolf in sheep's clothing

rebirth comes disguised as death,
a sharp edge to till me into the earth.

—*cocoon*

it's no surprise
your hero's a devil.
you sold your soul
for a place at the table
with thieves.

−it's not your world anymore

the bronze birthright stuck in your teeth.
years of mourning twisted around your spine.
loneliness is your cup,
drink.
there is no hope,
only yielding.
bow until your forehead touches dirt
and there's no risk of breaking.
tear your wants, your needs from barren soil
and leave them for the rats.
this is the legacy we give you.
we, the hard women,
heartbroken,
hard losses,
hark the song of despair.
take what you're given and
ask for nothing more.

—ancestral prayer, part one

what i do not need
is your limitation,
your fear of difference,
your brittle bones splintering beneath
the weight of my joy.

–*kindly fuck off*

the trees are leaning in
to watch you dig.
layers of death cast aside,
a taste on the tongue with no substance.
maybe if you pause you'll see
there are no treasures here.
you're all out of time
(and hunger)
—can you stop now?
can you lay down your shovel
and become someone else?

—gravedigging and other ways to fill the void

i have knots
where there should be rivers,
ropes wrapped around my bones
and in my teeth,
generations of silt settled
in drifts under my skin.
i strain and bleed
and find that only stillness
(and the moon)
can set me free.

−unnamed

this precarious tilt
leaning into the wind.
a slip into freedom
(or death).
what is liberty but opportunity
to fall, break, expand into the biting cold,
spiral nearer the sun 'til the wax drips from your not−wings.
it is a grave thing to ask for flight then fetter yourself,
a grave thing to be brought to the edge and become a stone,
a grave thing to put your hands around beauty and squeeze,
a grave thing to be handed a mirror and bury it.
the rot dissolves resolution,
progress cleaves muscle from bone.
we asked for wings and got instead
the whistle of the coroner's tools through night−dark skies,
the angry nonsense of old men more carrion than flesh
slurring their hatred over invisible frontlines
asking us to choose:
your child,
your self,
your blood,
your bones,
or theirs—
as though there was ever a difference.

−icarian peace

whatever the universe is made of
i am too much.
the hand that dug me out of the nebulae
was too generous.
i am all water
grasping at stones and leaving them smooth,
no purchase for my frigid fingers.

i dig in my heels
and make canyons where mountains used to stand.
i am still only for a season,
the cold crackling within
until thin rays release me.

−*overflowing*

do i get to be a golden thing
if my blood pools on your floor?
do i get to be precious and protected
if i'm also the monster under your bed?
let's say for a moment you're right
and i have nothing buried within
but shame and broken bones.
that i am the hungry void always asking
and never satisfied.
that i leave only grief and loss
in my wake.
i don't want to be
a petal floating in a stream
(a silent, beautiful thing)
my rage corked and aging.
i am the hurricane moving coastlines and
flattening shopping malls
and eating my way inland.
if you believed my teeth were sharp
you should have behaved better.
you shouldn't have clicked your tongue in disappointment
or crushed me under your god–fearing thumb.
i don't want to be like everyone else,
longing for the scales of justice to tip
enough for you to fall into the hell you made.
no.
i will be the final weight that pushes you over.
i will listen as the ancient gods recount your hubris.

i was a beast asleep until you shook me
(may that knowledge nail your coffin tight).
everyone else is holding their breath
to see what will become of you,
but i have written your ending.

−you know who you are

this fist is a map of
white knuckle moments and
stings better forgotten,
petals crushed and
stained skin.

 −*today i'm letting go*

i am sitting
(like you told me)
in the middle of myself
where the darkest things are rooted
asking the sharp shovel questions,
tired of protecting this fragile heart.
release me upon the world
to feel and grow and know
that no one is going to cut me
to a size that fits
inside their mouth
so they can spit me out
with their half-masticated
grievances and broken teeth.

-what can be done to fix me?

when i cut open
my ribs and let
all the birds loose,
i'll know (finally)
how the trees feel
in october.

−bare, clean, wrapped in the wind

we rubbed salt in our eyes because you told us to.

spread it over our tongues and wept

as you tilled it into the soil,

called it medicine.

too much of any good thing is poison.

(too much of you poisoned us)

we have preserved each of your lies

while you line marble walls and sodden tents

with your promises.

you taunt empty stomachs and preach

from the highest seats.

(our bodies are dust)

there is no justice for the least of these.

you have scorned our beauty

and replaced it with shame.

—what if we never escape you?

we are cracked deeply by our own thirst
sent here to reach our long arms
into the darkest waters
to pull you to safety.
seduced by the cool depths,
you plunged
'til the thought of breath bent you in half,
'til you could no longer feel the up and down,
'til your skin turned waxy gray and hollow,
'til you preached the gospel of the abyss like it was your own.
why do all your rescuers end
in shipwrecks and splintered bone?
maybe it is the sun's honesty you fear,
the unforgiving revelation in every shadow.
fear that we can see the blackened veins beneath your skin,
the lies that coat your tongue.
we wanted to pull you to the surface,
breathe into your lungs,
welcome you to shelter.
you writhe at the thought
and so we leave,
our own reflection the last we see of you.
leave you to bury yourself in untruths,
in chaos, in madness.

−we'll take our thirst over your certainty

which of these
will i regret
and which will
make me whole?

−*vices*

i forgot my lines—
the things i used to say
when you tightened
the ropes and asked
"does it hurt?"
(it did)
but you couldn't hear me then
and you sure as hell
don't hear me now.

—ghost

how can you sit on your hands
while their heart is falling
deeper into yours?
knowing the pain they feel
and swearing you mean
no harm?
(for you spoke no promises)
you kissed no lips
but your eyes
were always there,
asking if they'd like to take
a chance with you.

−regret is a bitter beast

burn your sad poems,
cut back your vines from my throat.
(we are separate)
you pull the joy from my belly
and swallow it whole.
(i cannot breathe)

−i am not therapy

learn which promises
to keep and which
were born of desperation
and the ticking clock.

−younger you did their best

i'm afraid that
i will always be
a black hole,
that nothing will fill
the gaping mouth within
and it will consume me whole.

−late night thoughts

maybe you asked permission.
(you don't need it)
maybe it's written on your palms
but you've forgotten how to read it.
maybe you knew once
or no one ever told you.

here's the truth:
you don't have to drink
from every cup you're given.

—martyr/saint

i've met her
in glimpsed reflections,
in evening shadows filled with fireflies.
she's marble, yes, and fire,
water flowing from her fingertips
when she chooses.
she channels storms and starlight,
collects deserts in her chest.
her mouth is lined with roses, thorns intact.
she has swallowed the universe twice.
you will not find the end of her,
she belongs to no one else.

−*mirror*

the load you carry
has never lined my back.
my skin has never known those teeth
or shed blood under the sole of that boot.

the boot is on my foot,
my teeth sharpened by
generations of pain
inflicted so that i could
stand atop a stolen land,
eating food i did not grow,
reading poems i did not write,
and swear that i want healing.

−remorse does not heal wounds

the cold gasp of air
is only the beginning.
waking up for the first time is painful.
(but so is everything else)

let that restless hum
(you know the one)
uproot the trees you did not plant.
make space for everything
your heart wants.
(yes, all of it)
you are yours
and this is yours
and spring comes every year.
(ready or not)

−i am so fucking glad you're alive

collapse the
stone-walled gardens,
dammed rivers,
smoking bees,
and bury them
deep inside
your ribs
'til you wake,
bursting forth
into coal-dusted
blooms.

—metamorphosis

the undoing
is a beauty all its own,
loosening ties
and pretense,
displaying bones
and sinew,
deep wisdom
open to the wind.

i am always this
but you do not always
choose to see.

—winter

sometimes the thorns are deep
and every pull drives them deeper.
every urge to run a cry
that dies in your swollen heart.
sometimes it takes a cut that nearly kills
to find the door.

—you must find the door

i've stopped writing and
started bleeding instead.
i haven't lost myself yet.
no.
i've found things no one
warned me about.
(and it's okay)
the lump in my throat
was fear last week
and now i'd swear
it's hope.

—i've always been more than i thought i was

today i am
collecting pebbles
          (and shadows),
digging in the dirt for sunshine,
pulling it up over my feet,
pushing down roots,
calling the wind.

today i am
becoming something
          (sharp and wild),
opening doors they said to leave shut,
burning the rot away.

—i've always needed less than i thought i did

"shed your skin."
like it's easy.
like the smallest movement
doesn't burn and pull and break
who i thought i was
into someone i don't yet know.
"shed your skin," they say.

−and i do

i got it from my mother.
she sent me, pockets laden with treasure,
healing in my fingertips.

it passed through the weathered hands
of my ancestors so i could bring some relief
to this place.

i saw your suffering
and sought wisdom to remove the weight
from your back, the boot from your neck.

if you were only willing,
i could show you how to hear the plants whisper.
how to take only what you need.
how to breathe yourself roots.

yours was a jagged-edged condemnation
of beauty you could not understand,
the heat of fire and fear.

now i am gone, my gift with me,
and you are free to reduce the earth
to cinder and soot.

−the monsters are men

the obsidian cut of deep sea at sunrise
is more than a mirror.
depth has its own light
shining in questions
pushed past the edges to
sink toes into muddy creek waters
and leave fractures in bedrock.
(level those greedy machines)
there's a place to catch
stars in glass jars
and make a home
in my own depth—
cavernous soul
in red lipstick
with lifetimes to share.
it's me.
i'm here.

—sparkling

the grit beneath my nails,
on my knees,
in my eyes,
is no more a mark of failure.
it's the triumph of a soul
who scaled mountains
with joy under her tongue,
who found truth in thunder
until her own heart
shouted the storm's song
from every precipice
and ascended with the echoes.

—my friend, the desert

i do not want your porcelain liberation,
your saccharine smiles,
sticky hands around my wrists,
the leash of your hunger.
who are you saving?
not me.
i'm happy here among the clouds.

−do not keep me from the sky and call it love

how can you distill your essence to a thimbleful
when you have carved canyons
and worn cliffs as a crown?
do not try to fit yourself into
someone's cupped hands.

they can become the sky,
the mountains,
whole continents.
(as they were born to be)
or they can watch
as you carry your treasures away
and leave no piece of yourself behind.

−pearls/swine

what does it feel like
to know you are the
before/after
upon whom
my life is
split?

−after is an avalanche

there's nothing more political
than the scars on your hands and
how i know them by heart.

−anarchy

the fire under your tongue
won't burn me up.
i am the rain, waiting
for you to speak the sun
into existence
again.

—balance

there is poetry in illness
(they say),
in the sparkle of shattered glass,
in tear stained cheeks,
in December sun
and May snow.
and i hope
(i hope, i hope)
they're right.

—spoiler: they are

the scream is sacred,
a feral prayer bouncing off the sky
when whispered pleas are not enough
and sunset feels like death.
let the mountains feel your agony
and the trees sway with your rage.
the blood moon holds vigil
for this beginning,
the womb of your new hope.
(welcome home)
the velvet dark will hold you well,
your not-beautiful and sharp-edged
knitted together—a creature of the night.
the owl does not judge
and the river flows whether you see it
or not.

-a new day

the bronze birthright solid in your hands.
years of labor twisting through your spine.
are you ready?
we have all drunk this wisdom
for your healing.
live.
bend forward into tomorrow,
until you're running with the wind.
tear our greed and failure from fertile soil
and leave them for the rats.
this is the legacy we give you.
we, the hard women,
heartbroken but learning
even in death,
hark this song of hope.
dream water where we saw
only gravestones in the desert.
and take us with you.

–ancestral prayer, part two

i think
   i could
      slip
until the cool water
covered my eyes
and carried away the
breathlessness
of life.
until my roots
were clean again
and i was free.

—river thoughts

with each day
i will unravel more
until all that's left of me
is wild and open,
glittering in the sun.

−*after the collapse*

remember
what it feels like
to see the dewey
milky way
spread across
a velvet sky.

—smallness isn't something to fear

this year i have a body you haven't touched.
every inch of soft skin free from your curses,
every organ filled with new hope.
today i am not her—
body unsullied by your greed and
a face lined with joy instead of grief.
i waited seven years to have eyes that never shed a tear for you,
to fill these lungs with anything but screams.
(i know you hear me singing)
(i hope it turns you inside out)

−2022 (i win)

stand reverently at love's door.
remove your tired shoes and
step into her aspen cathedral
so the honey sunlight
can spill across your skin.
in this soft place
(and holy)
you can grow roots
and let the earth whisper
sweet things
to you.
love will loosen
your cinderblock fists
and wrap your
scar tissue heart
in autumn leaves.
she will ask you to stay
and leave the door
swinging in the breeze.

—settle for nothing less

some of us have love

dripping from our fingertips,

running down our spines,

flooding every room in this fallen down house.

we're drowning in its ebb and flow,

praying for a buoy.

but there is only us

(marooned)

with so much left to give.

—what use is a love you can't breathe

one thing you must know:
i will make poems out of your hands
and pull starlight into your eyes.
i will make magic out of you
whether you deserve it or not.

—please, please deserve it

if we put our heads together
surely we can figure out how
to hold the universes
within each other
in open hands so
they can grow
(wild, sweeping)
while we dream.

−*is this living? it is, it is.*

i gave my love for real
every time. but it's
a living thing.
what started as one
slender tree is
now a forest.

—every leaf is yours if you want it

i will make many promises—
and swear to keep them all.
but this one is tattooed on my palms:
i want you big, breathtaking, devastating,
enough to drown me,
or not at all.

−100%

maybe the moon told me about you,
or i saw your smile in the sun.
all i know is seeing you
the first time
didn't feel like
the first time
at all.

−hi

if you stay,
if you keep the promises
you've whispered in the dark,
if you press in when
things are hard,
if you don't make me small
so you can climb on my back,
if you live honestly
next to me—
you will be the first.

−forgive my surprise

i want to write a stack of poems
about your lips,
your eyes,
your funny brain,
and the way you crack open
when you laugh.
i'll carefully polish each one,
bind them up gently,
place the whole thing in your beautiful hands,
and say
"here it is, my whole heart, all for you."
then you'd know for sure what this is.

−(it's love)

i've only been loved in fractions,

puzzling equations that reduced me by half,

half seen,

half formed,

half known,

(me minus me is palatable).

cut into pieces so i could be easily swallowed.

(i'm the kind of alive that gets stuck in their throat)

you've come without a knife

to drink deeply and draw constellations on my skin.

you're making maps and finding hidden places.

you peer into my depths unflinching,

worship my shadows and my sun.

the more you see, the more you want.

(and i'm ruined for anything else)

−speechless

your eyes
(warm like sunshine)
tell me everything i need to know.
fingertips on collarbones
and kisses softer than moonlight
sparking a million revolutions,
a big bang on your lips.

–oh no

i knew i would love you that day on the lake,
your face turned up to catch the frigid rain drops,
smile like the pines.
i knew i would love you,
i just didn't know how much or how long.

—some things we don't know 'til it's over

choose white knuckles,

apologies and thornless roses,

or a cool dip in a

clear pool on a hot day.

from a great distance

filled with sun or

in the shadows at dusk.

eyes wide open

or clamped shut.

an olive branch or

a smooth stone.

brown pie crusts and

worries in the dark.

with open hands

and feet buried in sand.

—there are a thousand ways to love someone

you are the sky,

stretching from ocean to ocean,

mountains reflected in your eyes.

rooted deep in dark soil,

singing sunlight to the stones.

the rain,

the wind,

the fullness of a summer stream,

the cracking of ice on a winter morning.

−sunflower soul

they will love you with your complications.
they will.
they will hold tenderly the parts of you that are
unwavering, exhausted.
they will love the person who lives beneath
the calluses of labor.
they will.
until then, darling, you can
(you must)
love the tender heart buried
where life sunk its hatchet.
love the you who still sees magic in moonlight.

−you are worth this and more

feel the rain on your face with me.
let's hold hands and watch every droplet hit the lake.
let's talk about the rainbow, the mountain,
your eyes, the way your skin feels on mine.
let the world move on without us.

–please

the blankets became mountains.
and you, tucked between,
sprouting wildflowers along your spine.
nestled under lightning and shadowed woods,
a meadow you carved for yourself
when hard hands, sharp tongues
left you gardenless, bereft.
now you drink from the coolest rivers
and sleep under moonlit skies,
listening to the soft music of your body whisper
thank you
thank you
thank you.

−sick day hymn

the body
(your body)
is a love letter—
a gasp of fresh air,
a spark in the darkness.
every curve and angle,
the parts you've altered
(beautiful)
and those you still cannot look in the eye
(beautiful).
it is the same as the earth,
the ocean,
venus in her orbit,
a galaxy expanding into space.
the universe in awe of itself,
a ubiquitous seed of wonder
planted in the expanse
and blooming now in you.

—if you cannot love it, at least (at least) let it be

this could have been
shy eyes met in a crowded room,
a friend of a friend of a friend,
elbows brushing in an airport,
a mumbled excuse me,
i'm sorry.
(hello)
a missed connection,
a brutal heartbreak.
two months too early,
a decade too late.
it could have been anything
(or nothing at all)
but what are the chances, my love,
that it could be this?

—*everything*

you are the rain in my desert.
precious, carefully savored,
a cool breeze after a blistering sun.
you leave life in your wake
and pull beauty from places
that were long thought dead.

−i cannot get enough

you reached into my chest
and pulled my heart into the sun,
a glittering, lovely thing.
you cradled it in your hands
with such tenderness and said
"look how beautiful you are."
i knelt there in that sacred place
to thank whatever gods brought you to me.
and then held your sparkling heart
as though it were my own,
(maybe it is)
in awe of you
and the gift you trusted
to my shaking hands.

−*what is this?*

let us sink our teeth into this,
wrap our arms around it
and just breathe,
give ourselves to it
and know it will give freely back.
the pain of love is a prayer
we will whisper into the night.
all the heart i have is yours.
i will hold a space for you
to breathe.
i will rejoice in your victories
and weep for your pain.

−if you'll have me

it's been a moon since i met you
(only one)
and already i've penned more poems
with your name than any other.
i blame the fever,
the drop of water on my tongue,
begging you to leave fingerprints,
a prism of desire wrapped
around my wrists.
(please)
leave crescents across my chest
and roses on my hips.
let them know i am yours,
and have been longer than
the stars remember.
ruin me for their
half-uttered admiration
and hollow praise.

—*yes, yes, yes*

i swear
i'd have known you
by any name
in any lifetime.

−heart of my heart

i woke up to a new world today,
one where my hand is tattooed
over your heart and i can
feel it beat no matter how far
away you are.
one where i can take a thousand years
to trace the planes of your face,
map out every scar and freckle,
remind you there are suns in your eyes.
(you radiant thing)
one where there's a greenhouse on my shoulder
and a cottage in my throat
where you can rest and grow—
all yours, only yours.
one where i wake up to you
and fall asleep to you
and meet you on the still waters of another life.
one where we give each other
clean breaths and dark soil and deep roots
and whistles and whispers and music
and more freedom than we dared hope for.
one where your voice is clear above the others
and we hold our silent space together
using only the moon to tell time.

−*confession*

i don't regret it,

the way i ran my fingers through your hair

and let you kiss my neck.

i don't regret the way my heart

opened to you,

the trust,

(the pain).

i don't regret letting you love me

or loving you back,

even if it was a flash of lightning

that burned us both up.

at least now i know

i can burn

after so long believing

i was only ash.

−thank you/i love you/i'm sorry

loving you was as easy as breathing,
quick like october.
we had hives fully of honey and
cellars of wine
waiting for someday.
now the space between us is vast
and we cannot uncross it.
i've released you to your future
and me to mine.
when the warm blanket of a summer night
finds you wrestling,
know that i am as altered as you
in the absence of this.
our love still exists today
somewhere
in the gravitational pull
of what we were
and what we may be in another life.

−it wasn't forever, but it was good

when soft no longer serves me
i'll become dark eyes at midnight,
broken glass in alleyways, and
the owl's funeral song.
who knows if it's a blessing or a curse?
(who knows if i'm a blessing or a curse?)

alone, i am a winged nightmare
sweeping through shadowed woods,
understood only by the wolves
on their winter hunt.
a horror to some, a goddess to others,
but wholly at home in myself.

−watch how easily i walk away when your knives come out

when i say i won't go quietly
i mean you'll feel the ache
in the shadows
where i used to live,
the loss of me in every
hollow space
i made you forget.
i'll burn nothing down
(leave no blood)
but you'll feel it just the same.

−the cost of loving me

i want to press my face against the sky,
hold the pebble of a sun,
inspect it like a diamond
and name all of its flames.

then i'll swallow it whole,
let it burn away yesterday,
take the shadows with it
and give me space to breathe.

−good morning

time adorns her fingers,
dangles on her cadent laughter.
(no rush, no hesitation)
she lifts the tides around her ankles
and tiptoes across mountain peaks
guiding us to hidden springs.
(drink deep and meet yourself anew)

-our sage, the moon

dead trees weigh heavy,

a star collapsing.

(the dark is alive, too)

so much effort

only to fall

short,

let down.

the moon still shines

in halves and quarters.

misstep,

mistake,

misspoken—

a soft place for new roots.

winter looks like death

until it doesn't.

—death looks like the end until it's not

if i could go west, i'd drink an ocean,
swallow it whole and ask for another—
let me be bottomless in my hunger,
voracious in my need.
i am so spacious it terrifies you.

my lover is the east—sculpted from soil,
sandstone eyes and juniper hands,
a mountain answering only to the slow
march of seasons and cool river tongues
who spent thousands of years singing
truth to his heart.

i gave birth to the north wind god,
questions and what–ifs strong enough
to shift a storm and tear trees from their roots.
great dreamer, dream us a better someday
put life into our sails and cut us clean
from the shore.

the south took everything
but left me crystalline, a prism
for the sun to speak rainbows to the ocean
and see his love up close.
i will show you yourself.
i will show you your broken bones
and the fire will weld you back together.

i am where the love goes when

there's nowhere left to put it.

your hands pass right through me.

the knives pass right through me.

i am so spacious it terrifies you.

i am the place the arrow calls home,

the deep hearth and warm bed,

the knowing that lives behind your sternum,

the arms that hold your grief when it becomes hard to breathe.

so spacious it terrifies even me.

−call the four directions and make your body home

go home.
pull the dark soil over your head
and sink deeply into the cool abyss.
clasp hands with the roots
and let them pull you deeper
into the heart of creation
where the sun is a whispered memory
and each heartbeat is a symphony.
instead of birdsong, take the slow rhythm
of the creatures of decay
sending new life
(and hope)
to a surface they'll never see.
go into the viscera of the mountain,
watch water build temples and
stones become portals.
even here in the dark, you burn,
proving there's little difference
between being buried and unburdened.

−take me with you

it's miraculous.
you across time and space
fully a child,
fully wrinkled by time,
existing in every phase,
effortlessly holding all life's lessons in your bones
and yet you want me to believe you're mortal,
that there are no stars under your tongue.
i would be a fool not to see.

−you terrible liar

the yous in yesterdays, past lives, other planes
bow to this you here today.
universe meets body,
nature at play,
more colors and dreams
in an eyelash
than fit in most stomachs.
the grieving mourning in your backbones—
not-here and too-soon sculpted your face
but did not make it to your heart.
your heart is kept,
joy-cocooned new beginnings
wrapped around your sternum,
dripping with Jupiter's radiance
(all of space is yours),
the doors of Janus at your elbows
(all the roads are yours).
knots unwound into i am's,
a drumbeat for dancing.
i am.
i am.
i am.
you will always be
held gentle and safe
by hands that bring only freedom
to be and
to know yourself and
to shout your knowing from mountaintops

and movie screens

and every page your pen touches,

to see yourself in the mirror

and kiss your lover on a sidewalk,

to drink deeply of everything good

until it runs down your chin

and you're gasping

(laughing)

for air.

you will be surrounded by people who deserve you.

we will build a world that deserves you.

−for my trans loved ones, a blessing

if it's the sacred
you're looking for,
open the window and
let the sun filter in.
look in the mirror and
let love be the
first word on your lips.

−holy

the dark sky is abundant
with secrets waiting to be discovered.
only those who sit
with their ear to the earth,
their eyes on the stars,
who are still long enough to hear
the song of far away planets,
the whisper of wisdom's muse—
only they will know.

−blessed are the patient

i held the moon
here in my hands
and asked her
please
to bend the world
if only a little.
and she laughed
and said
"dear one, how can i
when it's there in your pocket?"
and i looked
but my pockets were empty
except for the breath i'd been
holding too long.

-even this is significant

my sliver of a soul
and thundering heart,
the skin that holds me
from cleaving in two,
lips as adept for love
as for cursing your name—
i forgot that these
(that i)
am a monument
to the sacred.

−let yourself live, my love

never small enough,
bent over heart–holding
turtle shell almost home
in a wasteland that
could have been more
but was razed for
someone else's dreams.
you were very brave
with throat shut tight.
no one heard your heart
beat in the madness,
the smallest one
forgotten.
but I can hear you now
in your cape with the trees,
singing your voice raw
and telling stories
to the fairies,
bare feet,
bare bones,
bared teeth,
like the wolves taught
when they licked your wounds.
there are no walls that would hold you,
no roof to block out your sun.
i'll watch little footprints on muddy paths,
tuck you under moss
when the moon whispers

"good job today,"
and leave you
to the beauty of your
dreams.

−*thank you, little one*

you will find
you need both spring
and winter.
time to rest
and time to bloom.
when one season ends
and another begins,
let time carry you
and rhythm do its work.

−child of the earth

when you step,

the earth kisses the soles of your feet.

the sun rises to see your face.

and the moon?

she moves oceans to carry you

wherever you'd like to go,

in this plane or the next.

−you are the universe reaching for itself

gather your not-afraid,
your not-lonely,
your not-ashamed.
fill your pockets with pebbles and
build forts in the field that stand like temples
to the liberation of joy,
maskless pleasure,
unbroken spirit.
tell your secrets to the trees
and link arms with nature's beings while
your bare feet drum the rhythm of the seasons.
kiss the earth and sleep under the stars,
make rainbows from creek water,
let yourself be loved and known and wanted.
let them close enough to inspect the
freckles on your nose and the scars on your knees.
no bad weather, bad dreams, bad you.
spread your arms wide enough for the mountains,
wide enough for the sea
(hold them free).
peace peace.
sing peace to the mother,
sing peace to the sky,
sing peace to your hidden self.

−before i met god

i want to write you a poem,
make it a salve to protect you
from the wind and sun.
instead i am pressing together
words without meaning,
holding unlit lanterns in the dark
(i do not believe in a better world).
but you are here.
i see your face when i close my eyes
and it feels like medicine.
the world may never hide its teeth,
but you will still be
watching the sunset,
holding my hand,
asking questions
i do not have answers for.

−thank you for being here

do not subsist on someone's thin love.
do not sit at their feet asking to be seen.

you whole, beautiful soul,
you absolute ocean,
you are your own soft bed,
your own sunshine
(and blue sky),
an abundance within.

do not settle for bones
when you were made for slow feasts,
for kind eyes in the mirror.

—unstoppable force & immovable object (you are both)

you can have the sun,

the glittering rain,

all the flowers, every tree.

snowy mountains tucked under your chin.

oceans cradled in your arms,

planets wound into your hair.

every star aligned along your spine.

a mouth full of fireflies, of thunder.

—just ask

hide me in a mountain
cradled by canyons
ancient and solid,
untouched by the fire,
washed clean by the rain.

–and leave me there

i want kisses pressed
into my palm,
words dripping
off your chin and
into my mouth.
the stars in my eyes
reflected in yours,
fingerprints dusted
in shadows.

−is it too much to ask?

press your nose to the glass,
let the mycelium of your breath
weave into the fog,
watch it drift away
on an invisible breeze.
look deeply beyond,
into the not—here and not—now.
allow yourself to see
what lies buried,
the ancient mysteries within.
relax into the space between heartbeats
and leave the trail behind.
move through the shadow,
become the secret thing.

—*veil*

at the precise moment of bursting,
the tearing of seams,
(you will not break).
the universe is taking a breath
and you are expanding
to hold all the wonders and aches
within your belly where
they will turn to flowers
(or fireworks).

−it hurts, i know. hang on

i've come a long way
through the darkest nebulae,
hidden in the earth
'til the rain called
me forth.
the sun smiles upon me,
but the moon is my dearest friend.
i am both here with you
and there with her
and everywhere in between.

−torn between two worlds

be very still.
allow that last lingering thought
to drift away.
watch yourself
find safety in the space within
(a universe of possibility, unparalleled power).
seize this sacred moment,
treat yourself as precious.

-deep breath

i've built a home of light.
blue for my open-sky soul,
green for sleep in mossy glades,
gold for sun, silver for moon,
black for the night-velvet sky,
red for the love wrapped around my fingers,
purple for the lilacs in my hair,
orange for every burst of joy between my ribs.

i have no need for armor and weapons
i am the sea, the wind, the trees—
my soul untouched by your shame.

whatever sticky madness you carry cannot reach me.
it will not bring me harm or leach the light from my eyes.

—may all your arrows fly straight back home

what do you see from there,
dear friend?
is it fire or forest,
rain or wilting sun?
when you blink,
it will change.
bury your feet in the earth,
reach out to the sky
and wait.

−all of this will pass

you are big enough
(spacious soul)
to hold all this pain
and joy together,
to know nothing
and everything
all at once.

−tension

in time blindness and moon months
and years of no sun, a shift
smaller than a snail shell.
eyes in dark corners,
edged in red–rimmed hail marys,
cigarettes between chapped lips,
laughter borne here
on the back of a mother
and buried in the garden.
flowers turn their gentle faces
toward a stifled sob of grief
and the earth turns with them.
joy is a shadow on a branch
looking like something else
not–quite–here, not–quite–now,
a rendition of a borrowed thing.
new ideas aflame, in love—
a steady–on to exoskeletons and camouflage
and hands that do not scar the earth.

–blessed are the freaks

the moon does not
resist her phases
nor the trees
the shedding of their leaves.
there are many ways
to move forward.
flow like water
making your own way,
wearing down mountains,
carrying only what's
in your hands.

−take note

blessed are those
who do not blink against the snow,
who stand, chest out,
and stare down the burning sun.
they coax water out of rocky soil,
and climb the same mountains
that once bled them,
insisting that tomorrow is a promise.
(not a threat)

−the longing is survival

show me your gritted teeth,
your broken skin,
the ringing in your ears.

here is where you find it.
(lean in gently)
take yourself by the hand
        and heal.

—you need love/not fixing

stretch out your hands
unfurling petals,
invite the cold rain,
pinpricks on skin.
let the frost burn
and retreat into
the warm earth.
rest until you're ready
to spring forth
and climb toward the sun.

−begin again, begin again

i cannot tell you
how often i forget
that i carry
safety within me.

—where the wound is

this is the tiny death
before slumber,
a final burst of sparks
as fog obscures
the waning sun.
let fire swallow
decay you've carried
in your bones.
rest here in the shadows
and, please,
let yourself be.

−it's not forever

because you were taught that love is a knife
you believed your commitment could only be
measured in blood.
what do they need?
(cut)
who do they want me to be?
(cut)
are they happy?
(cut)
because you were taught that love is a knife
you learned to hold yourself hostage,
to sacrifice yourself,
pouring out your essence to a hungry god's
blind eye and stone heart.
but i'm telling you that love is not a knife.
love is the wings you didn't know you had
until your feet left the ledge.
it's a warm breath suspended in fog on a cool day,
the gentle phases of the moon,
a needle and thread
(to mend).
it's palms open and turned to the sky,
it's laughing
and gasping
and hoping
and praying
and having.
it's everything,

everywhere.
it's you.

−bury the knife and don't mark the grave

Acknowledgements

This book took five years of deep healing to write and I'm so grateful to finally pass it onto you. There are a lot of mentions of the moon and nature. There are a lot of *i's* and *you's* (they're me and you and all of us). There are a lot of big feelings I've attempted to distill so I can breathe. Thank you for having patience with all of it. The moment you read a poem, it ceases to be mine and becomes yours. I hope the ones you need find you. You're doing amazing and I'm so glad you're here.

To Myla/Mylo—thank you for being a shining example of what it looks like to live authentically. You inspire me everyday to keep growing and healing and loving this wide world. And thank you for doing all the illustrations on the cover and throughout the book. I love you, angel face.

To my mom, Axel, JD, and Gianna—I'm endlessly grateful for the privilege of living this life with you.

To Sarah—your talent and support and kindness are awe inspiring. Thank you for being the world's best editor and an even better friend.

To Shannon—you're the best copilot for every adventure. Thank you for saying "yes" to my dreams and cheering me on. I'm so grateful to be on this journey with you.

To Forrest—thank you for challenging me to write better and longer pieces until I found new parts of myself. And thank you for inspiring me with your own vulnerable creations.

To Becca—thank you for being with me through so much growth and change. I'm so grateful.

To the QFFCC—thank you for sharing your beautiful creative genius and pushing me to grow.

To Jess Zimmerman—*Women and Other Monsters* blew my world wide open and inspired the title of this book. Thank you.

About the Author

Kaela Prall is a writer and poet with a keen eye for storytelling. Her work reflects her passion for healing, liberation, and community as well as her perspective as a queer, neurodivergent woman. She resides in Colorado with her teenager, their two beloved dogs, Harley and Rainy, and one clever cat, Skromby.

Her debut poetry collection, *Rupture and Repair*, was published in 2019. Her second solo collection, *Chimera*, published in 2024.